ants moving the house millimetres

ants moving the house millimetres
nadine botha

ISBN: 0-9584915-1-8

deep south
p.o. box 6082
grahamstown
6140
www.deepsouth.co.za
contact@deepsouth.co.za

We gratefully acknowledge financial assistance for publishing this book from
The National Arts Council

deep south titles are distributed by
University of KwaZulu-Natal Press
www.ukznpress.co.za
books@ukzn.ac.za

Some of these poems have appeared in New Coin, Botsotso, Writing from Here,
Aerial, www.donga.co.za, www.southernrainpoetry.com, www.litnet.co.za
and www.sweetmagazine.co.za

Cover Painting : Colijn Strydom
Cover design : Nadine Botha
Text design : Paul Wessels
Layout : Martin Hiller

contents

Keep left

Excuse me,
I have left the room.

Sorry about the empty glass,
might have to empty the ashtray.

The hint of what you think
you smell

is probably in your mind
but I'm there too.

And I might not have been,
if it weren't for that.

The bus prick and his doos

The bus guy,
wet gently combed hair –
sautéed carbon monoxide –
in wheeled prowling pad.

I watch him,
watch his chicks,
clumsy hawk denying a vulture.
He watches pencil boxes

of weeks waiting
for the write time.
He pounces it on a day
there is no one pencil box,

"Nice pencil box."
He'll say she was intrigued
by his attendance.
She, repulsed

by his slight grinning
tum tum checked shirt
looks like a machine, smiles.
She ignores –

"I'd like a pencil box like that.
Where did you get it?"

Unpoetic things

I went to buy an alarm clock today.
Walked into a large department store,
filled with practical things.
Like pots.
And suitcases and fluff removers.
And braais and self-cleaning plates.
And toilet mats and reusable toilet paper.
And running shoes and bicycles.
And umbrellas and inflatable swimming pools.
I love shops like that.
I love shops that you can stumble around
looking for the rafters.
Even if you don't need rafters,
you can always buy a ladder.
Even if you don't need help,
every shop assistant stands.
In your way and smiles.
Every shop assistant stands and smiles
and nods.
As though they know
that you know,
exactly where to go.
To find the alarm clocks in the jewellery department.
Which I did, incidentally.
After asking for help.

Two-eyed because one is closed

Round mirror palette,
you point yourself pink
like a cat.
Demoned you say,
handing off your genes
down your pants
bril, din, like inter-language puns.

Posed like pussy make-up
on your face is a canvas
you kyk/cake taste
on your own piece of warm
subtle, washes your brow
splotched in line 6B
marked by the tip of a green

wean of framed
asbestos-curled paint images,
down the point of my Bic-faced ass
in this chair, you're staring at me
with your back, writing a self-portrait
painted by my eyes
is the two-backed beast.

Sleep simply alone

Inside a house
I have never been to,
you've moved your bed
right up to the computer.

But bugger all that you say,
you just want a mat.
You say it reverently with a pause
before the next drag.

I watch this again
you have said this
and I watch this again
your eyes dart, what?

Nothing.
I've reminded you before.
I remember.
I wonder about your memory.

You don't spend this much
time with any person.
It's almost a year now.
Your party tricks run out,

not your mind, ticks ticks ticks.
It really does.
In that silence of three weeks.
I wait for a call from you.

Then you can't wait anymore.
It's every day, it's every hour.
And it's not about feet.
It's the languidness of our voices

and our metaphysical connection.
We giggle again.
Again we fall over
each other, again.

Again I ask
if we repeat,
recycle,
rejuvenate, I know now

when you are going.
I feel relieved.
I feel guilty now
for not making it back to you.

The beating hump of witless arousal

In the same room on a day that is a Saturday,
I feel Saturday, I say lying
on the newspaper there is sand in my eyes
and nets around our bodies, talk of liaisons.
I see through my stoned eyes his lips
talking to my skin and I feel sentimental.

The cuntline in the rope of our legs,
thighs like sails and breasts like pirates,
it's a sailor's splice and a tautening of vows.
It's in the mist with your fingers in the wind.
Netted. Caught.
And released.

In this mutinous state
I want to enslave you.
Your clammy nipple in my nose,
hands hanging out of my anus and vagina –
handcuffs that fit
the ocean of hyperventilation in my ears.

Worker hives

I'm scared of my barefoot bees
flying my room at night.

I am not sweet – it's a secret –
sweating my white camisole

red with the hormone
smell of my curled traveller.

Lifting the floundering B,
leg mesmerised by its own death

drunk from white light –
thanks Edison!

Lifting the sting to the bin
on a piece of waste paper,

after carving it with paper cuts
I close the curtains.

Sleeveless goosepimples

Ants moving the house millimetres,
I shipwreck on the carpet
floating on hives and nests.

Coagulated and oil spattered
like an overblown chicken,
I have the music on.

Missing letter

One tobacco leaf,
a broken pipe
and the leftover hash.

Six condoms,
baby powder,
unopened KY jelly,

and the knife I wanted to kill you with.
Your fingers,
my love,

the death of me,
the space we shared,
my cum –

not yours –
and the abstractness,
I send you.

Spill

Mark my body
for I am
written on
my body
being unspoken.
Everything is
a sign
in this pocket
of lovely I'll
tell you if
you're always
around.

Runners

Rush hour in Harrismith is on foot.
The streetlights are on, but the sun's not down.
Air sings about missing the summer.
Pets are like water features.

And in small towns, they all run so fast.
Sport is still a utopia and I have a beer –
a sore sight to sorry eyes
structured around the TV.
I see my life as an excuse.

This is not my style

Today I went to girls high.
I took photos of the head girl.
Awkwardly posing in romantic interludes
with the head boy of boys high.
She probably thought we were koeks.
Collin came with me.
We kept using words like pastoral, haughty...
trying to start convention conversation,
make them relax and talking rich.

Strange it looked the same.
A cleaner, neater version of the same.
The same as I sit here
tripping to Sonic Youth's Ginsberg.
The same swooshing hoover phonics from Charles St.
The bedside lamp clamped to my bookshelf
and me in my camisole with my beer boep.
Lame armed writing striding through the paper
with distant desire for desire –
not this abstract pensive persistence –
trying to leash my tangible creativity
from my emotional dessert.

Dessert I say as though it doesn't feel
like the post-course lethargy of
Sunday afternoon and cheap vanilla sorbet
with bits of ice that taste like nothing.
And the couch numbness is my heart
while my eyes stream down my face at Frida,
even though it was bad, I told Collin afterwards.

I ran into him.
Outside the movie theatre.
He was lurking.
Hoping Jaco would come out.
I thought I was going to start crying

if I spoke to him any longer so I agreed
to have a cigarette with him.
I thought he had been crying too.
In Frida.
I don't know if he had been, but he wasn't in Frida.
I don't know which of us was more depressed.
My throat felt was suffocating me.
And I felt, feel, so empty.
I said I feel Stephan slipping
through my lips with my vacancy.
I have nothing to tempt him with
as sex has become the orgasm he can give me
and a landscape I can't even recall.

So I choose the path of least resistance
to get sex with him.
I even forgot that phrase when I spoke to him
last night, naked, my neck hanging
my head off the end of the bed.
Him lying on my pillows.
My legs around his waist.
A Rorschach test.
If it was a silhouette.

He switched off the light.
I put on my fishnet dress.
We fucked again until I was dry.
He wanked over my feet.
I lay there blank with vermicelli bliss.
Like a cake. A koek.
White on white like the moon
when we went outside, I tripped
over the perfect circle of chairs.
Inspired.

He walked into the dark of the garden
and came back having left.
I slept with lucid cummings offering pillows.
I wake rested.
But am too unmotivated to get up.
For what should I be at work at eight

if I can only start later.
For what stay at home awake
if I have to go to work.
For what work
if I might as well be dead?

This twisted feeling of almost angst

Self-prying abilities
of (s)talking.
How do you make snow stay
like love
you can never keep it('s)
in your hands.

I don't see them in my eyes really

Smooth like tiredness
clipped from a straw,
naivety sips milkshake.

From the glass booth
of the smoking section,
he holds her hands.

Their genitals are as visible
to me as to them,
in their eyes they hold a shyness,

to their ears.
In green with pink
and silence from where I sit.

While

Reflect in stillness
when all else gives in,
whisper yourself to me.
Enshrine my ear.
There's weight behind words
and looks between spaces
but the Morse-code is lost on me.

Goodnight to my sandwich

Gravity pulls the tomatoes from my buds
climbing into your cigarette.
Feeling. Air. Pressure. In your cheeks
recreating a John Cage.
But the suction. Fluxion.
Just. My squeeze
of a filter
just my filter
singe my fingertips as my ovaries whine.
Rough. Gums. To torpid tongues
raucous glurps of water.
Stomach. Choirs. Words
the hollow palate of sucking.

I'm not there to visualise

Digital yellow
one candle died,
a couple did.

Cream on winter snow,
up against blue
and silhouettes.

The door is painted.
A square and
rumble

on pink lit carpet.
Up from the
ground,

toes on speckled
bumps together
paper stompies

and sharp lines.
Clipped on, notice
your own

unwriting yourself.
In a spiral, you dreamt
a bucket stuck on tiredness.

Still

White noise is turned
up my tingling nose nothing.
Without the constriction in my stomach,
throat trickles down my gut
ends in my anus
of non-phallic proportions,
of my existence spent nowhere.
My life is my future, is a computer.
Rat-mazed electrical circuits
brainwashed with omo
superbrite is her eyes.

In the sunshine of my glimpses,
the fingers of gods
painted in renaissance masterpieces
are all geoid, but not earth.
Shaped is what the brain is not wanting.
The brain is pink to the purple
degree of photons before it turns
into ultraviolet before it turns
into X-rays before it turns
into nuclear rays

fragmenting the disintegration,
the persistence, of memory.
Consciousness relies on being
numb to the awareness of feeling
my blood pump,
making my toenails grow,
even though I don't watch them.

I live in the capital

I live in the capital.
I've started this before,
it feels so normal.

In my mind it's just streets,
that I don't know yet –
compared to coming home

and McChicken
and Captain Copman.
Compared to not eating tuna or chocolate.

I feel so normal –
like not drinking beer
not having a car.

It doesn't feel like the capital.
But I am absurd.
So I'm still the same –

as sweet as your mother's friend,
or your friend's mother.
Living down the street,

I sculpt junkie lies
I pick up in drinking.
This is not the capital.

I live in the capital.
But politicians don't need to be sincere,
they just need good advisers.

When I think binary and do the opposite

The walls like red paint, are glass
in this abode I wave like a goldfish,
and breathe.
With my one hand trailing,

cotton string burning,
my ankle in step.
Callisthenics I try, to keep my brain alive,
so dislike it

like the sound of shutting dustbins.
Or marinating chops to the sight
of a man on the toilet.
Not someone – too personal.

Not a woman – too sexual.
I live in the habit of abstinence of what I don't know.
Know in the sense of empathy.
Empathy in the sense of psychoanalysis.

Psychoanalysis in the sense of non-judgmental.
Non-judgmental in the sense of unethical,
but for the ten commandments!
I write as though I'm a personals listing.

Except that would be the first to go
in a world where my choice was genius.
I would be a commoner,
and don't think I'd miss the loneliness.

Like an abstinence sufferer
I will always find virtue.
As opposed to the doubled big five
I don't know I've ever seen outside of dice.

I sleep.
Dream the door is locked,
and wake
not knowing any better.

I sleep again with reluctance
to wake.
I can make the sun rise
and crawl my eyes

in stripes,
I am black.
And white is the fathom
this.

Remembering something I lost when I wrote this

The highway is overhead this time.
We're at a petrol station.
You don't know how to react
to condoms on the highway.
I drop my head,
piercing the glance away
from us
are others.

We show ourselves to
blotch the paper, I recall
the last
moment in this moment,
dragging across the tarmac.
And a troop of hounds,
half jammed door.
My skirt in my legs.

Blood pouring my side
is alive
pumping gas,
petrol, no smell.
Smoking.
And not in the car.
Tugged tug
like a boat.

Fed this,
it's easy.
Rattles in a dark kitchen.
Flipping feet.
Posed fingers.
Shoes in hand.
Bright across the N3,
my skirt between my knees.

And blue sky
flat on my head.
Pieces below.
Landing.
Up in this
here.
I'm stumstruck,
I remember from the last.

The next level of pornography is taking the photo so you're looking at your own body

The twilight
said the freckled piano teacher,
penist teacher I said today it should be called,
was what Adorno ascribed as the ailment,
she didn't use these words of being conscious
the instant before losing yourself
and for an instant
being a bat AND yourself,
I use in this moment of my genitals
alight with presence,
she cut them I think
for that,
or maybe for the sunrise –
perpetually just above the horizon.
In my midday I talk about routes and my heart
is thumping to a rhythm of sex in his voice,
I expect,
so I hear it.
I feel it in a twilight of revulsion in my genitals.
Turds was the word I used the whole day –
not in relation to my genitals.
But it's twilight and the candle lubricated for a fuck,
she didn't fuck.
I didn't understand that I was aroused,
in myself disgusted, and thinking
that my association, my associate had raped me
by the instance in my head
I was not involved in but only on the outside,
could I watch it alone,
manifests fists in my life
I beat myself with
but never win.

Sexless

I shaved my pubic hair today in an act of mutilation.
I held my body on the bath rim,
clenched my teeth at my straining neck –
people are not ostriches that stick
their own head in their hole.

Henry Miller says it's ugly sexless, woman is bush.
I've never seen my sex since I was twelve and now
I am sexless with a mini-penis protruding from my thigh.
I feel the edges against my gauze underwear – is it? – was it?
As though I've claimed it now in my sexless sex,

I can draw curls and remember that I was,
and I am, feeling the seam of embroidered flowers
like legs in stockings, I am dehumanised
to patina of overture on sensation of sheath.
I am more than a shaft caressed by my clothes

on-off for sex as though it's romantic,
when it's a connection,
through a moon that is public property
in the fingers of my eyes,
I had to show someone.

Hoarfrost skull fluff

The last time I dyed my hair,
some fell out.
I had scabs on my skull –
like the Fanta ad.
I walked around with olive oil
doek op my kop – met die helm gebore.
Sat in the shade to avoid cerebral fries –
a tomato too short for French fries and salad head.

But when I cut off the dyed twangs,
my slowly recovering receding hairline
was far more than a kopdoek case.
I was a boy.
I dressed as a drag queen once.
Have never had such hot male attention.
Now as my styleless style gains in length,
I still haven't used a brush in six months.

But I can also make myself look like Laurie Anderson.
I do, in private and pretend I'm famous.
Contemporary aesthetic genius.
I also put on my old lime-green school dress.
I do it in private and don't tell anyone.
Not even Laurie.
Because I am Laurie.
And besides, we already share follicle secrets.

But most of the time, I just sit and stare at a blank page.
She probably also has that secret.
Or I cast Monty Python with Sartre's lobster men.
Laurie probably doesn't.
Not until I wrap the sushi in rice paper,
put it on the conveyor belt,
and squint eyelashes at fluorescent lights.
To see refraction.

But not a single one of my hairs —
even if there's always at least two
people in a room
with the same amount of hair on their heads —
warms the cold fish.
For my hair is not isolated to my head.
In fact, I shed like a reptile.
Especially, when I think I'm in a fishbowl.

We go to bed every night with it

With a voice like that you could save millions
if you sang.
No one listens.

Headaches are eased by coffee, Bill Gates once told me
that the adrenaline breaks up what's in your head.
I wasn't dreaming.

He was a waiter in my house.
When the shadow lifted he stumbled in,
I went to work.

At work they started a rumour that Bill Gates had been killed.
Five times.
Everyone fell for it.

Five times.
I took a pill.
Drank water.

I still have a headache.
I can't save.
No one can.

What we talk about when we talk about love

We lay naked in a single bed.
Talking.
Untouched as flesh.
I wanted you.
Clamoured all over you.
I wanted anyone
to tell me my head,
not in the clouds.
But we talked about
love and the like.
What it was, what it meant,
what other people had, what they wanted,
what we wanted.
But we couldn't say.
I never had it.
You've had it.
I asked you
if you ever tried to analyse our.
Fucked-up non-relationship. You said no
but started to then.
I tried to stop.
You.
I never had.
Didn't want.
Don't know if you stopped.
But we'll be okay.
We'll find what we're looking for –
we're content with the search.
Not to settle.
For always.
We scepticise the truths absolutes.
We don't see to come true.
I have my parents, you have yours.
We both have friends
and philosophise ourselves to shit.

Sex is with another person, everything else is spellbondage

You're-on my bath
on the edge-shirtless and
washing-me
like I'm-yours

and my vaginal-discharge is
distributed by-my fluxing
thighs you raise my-elbow,
bite-it,

wash my-armpit-I want to stop.
Come.
Stop coming.
Come again.

Come all the-time.
Because-you're right
here washing me back-then,
I think I-must be

dreaming the arousal.
I like arousal.
I could be aroused
all-the time

if it weren't for-sex.
But you're in the water.
We're in the water
cradling the-parabodies

of my own-bath,
I pull-you inside
like you-belong,
my discharge-doesn't,

it's just-a sidekick
I feel-now of the last time
I-simulated this
with-nothing

and now I do-too.
But-yet. It sits.
I sit in the bath. I-wait.
I look-at the white

tiles-again de-cleanse me.
The dog-prints,
my bitch, you-spank
me with my own-shoe

I am my-Cinderella,
not yours,
not your shoe
I I I I-breathe

but can't-forget.
Don't assimilate.
Don't want to.
Would-you?

We shouldn't create ourselves

Metaphysical stories
punch you in the face,
reality is just fixed.
Judy taking the bitch.

The puppets flock.
Fucked by what they're watching,
anal – Mr Sock
peeling designed for the onion metaphor.

I take the metatext
to the constable
sheriff in a small town,
where it doesn't make sense either.

At least it's not supposed to there.
While here, on my nose,
perched like slipping periscopes,
the mirror.

She regrets what is lost,
although she doesn't know what that is.
But it reminds her of the new place.
Of the old place, she remembers

it depressed her.
Shale off my shopping list.
Everything becomes evil,
living in the turnstiles.

I am young in love and full of scruples

There are bits on you, like limbs,
I wrap myself in like the fractal
of a marijuana plant that I watch
through bars, even though I'm on
the same side like the random
throw of continuity that I cannot
explain for your limber timbers
embroiling me in the weight
of a blanket and a duvet
too short for winter,
my bed is only hot when you're in
it but the sweat is precursing

the summer.
You're present. When you're here
and absent when you're not.
I don't know what to say
on the phone but love
is not the great conversationalist.
It's going down on me in my period
and tying my hands
to my neck with my scarf,
while you trace the lines
of my stockings
like limp used condoms

with no cum
you extract my legs and
spring brings blossoms and pimples
and uncomfortable trickles
on red-stained bras
from washing them in a bath
where lights melt with darks
and whites beam from winter legs –
unshaved jungles of mysteries
and the future.

I also think of the pleasure of merely being used

I can't stop thinking about sex.
Sex between my lips,
sex in my eyes.
Lips between
my lips in my labia
around a penis hard
between my finger sucked
on my nipples against
coarse hair in
my mouth sucking
balls popping from
my lips part for
gasp is muffled by
tongue down
my back fingers
dig slip slide
on sweat down
the crack in the sponge
of an ass explored
fingers feeling dark
but red in the eyes opening
to look to push
breasts around a penis
throbbing jabbing
my vagina the first
time deflated crammed
front-to-front gazing
up or down at a back
don't know where
to put my hands
slipping holding distracting
the foreskin against
my G-spot clitoris rupturing
on thrust harder more
I thrust too
am breathing too

fast too
think the shivers
the trembles
the weak
the knees
the last
fleeting scrawl at capturing
the eternity tension
is gone.
Slipped out.
Last gasp.

No second hand CO_2 to breathe.
Wet on the tongue left to lick.
Dry on the fingers left to feel.
Red on the eyelids left to black.
Only smell.

Cry Kerouac companion

Sheens of machinery
fish dead shadows,
saw dust-memories.
Front-door – broken off –
inside plants lint sleeve-witness.
Talk-about-it, drew the robe-
cone-fireplace: smoke stains
and open upside down,
quietly-unheard-unconscious.
Tracing needlepoint-nothing-metaphors
touching back –
buttons and tears, like lemonade-
job-trouble kitchen tulips.
Head-mouth rushed to fingers
looking (like) hunger-stricken-government,
educated-job laughing lopsided across-garden.
Tin-ring-evening-apron speaking paraffin-sweat-breath-skin
standing (like) clear escarpment-
functioning entrance-tent's exile.
Phone-small-scraps escape
sanitation-paratroopers, satellite-
relatives and active-networks.

Next time

We walk away.
Trying to find our underwear,
discarded, in dingy corner conversations
we didn't notice, in the silences.
Until we have to break.
Through each other's personalities
again. When you knock.
On my daily routine, with polite comments
about the process of dressing.
For the occasion of us walking.
Taking me back to school grounds smelling
rotting swill power games.
Badge wearers, light-headed.
Without weights.
Below, their names fading into my silence,
at the thought of the arbitrariness,
of your shoeless feet.
Walking across my scattered hooks.
When you just smile,
at the goodbye to nothing said.

I asked myself

I'm in this room, sleeping bag and a window.
In a biggish town with streetlamps –
and my undies – a meenthuis, no trees.
Streetlamps shine through the window.
I'm lying on the floor thinking if I drink
I will feel it – nothing.

My mother has been rhapsodising about why
I have to procreate.
How memes mean nothing without genes.
How we're tribal – our minds seek souls.
So I must live out her line.
I am an extension of her thoughts.

If she killed herself, she'd let the side down.
Her father was a carpenter and mother deaf.
My father is Afrikaans.
I mustn't let the side down by stepping out.
She says she failed me
if I don't have success in a relationship.

I drove fifteen hours with her today to her new life.
Glutted on my fantasy and disillusionment,
while it meant so much to her
because you're mine she said,
I asked her:
Do we really think the same?

Others' stories are anecdotal

Stomach kicked by the feathered
carpet in semi-transparent tops
spinning the revolution is happening
regardless of any functional tonsillitis
lighter smoker poker in the intestine
my being abstaining from feasts
fast furious fission facts true-story
boys in green hair on pimpled
staircases of long-legged knobbed
knees knowing parts growing
flowing faking this throw of words
tossed like a salad on a couch
my penal purpose absconded
with violent yearnings forgotten
dreams I think I had
I carry on in this seam so-ed for nine
on squared number, neat,
neatly squared off and blocked
blocked, I rummage the kitchen
cupboards rummage them again
for a forgotten joint forgotten
dream I write and write these words
fitting like one-armed bandits
on and over I pull the lottery
with a set of combinations run
dry and the meaning never does
relate beyond epiphenomenalised self
world needs a dictator to fit
the misfits to cherries, nanas
and oranges with Gay-Glo highlight
glass offices and polystyrene phrases
of whiteboard phases
white on black
and that was that this black
whiteness run away horizons
like mirages the view now is killing,
me like a tired philosopher cynical

of their utopia no future in this pen moment
with the same symbols
I still never can never could
will remember or cry
about what I wanted to say
in that robot stop sign
traffic pain, sun sore, eyes weep
in sweat is now – that's now
the relations of time whore as daily
my memory whores me
daily
but the then panopticon
who's the client pen aching
mind fixing faxing faking,
the notion of gesture here
emoticons there
we do not contain our actions
but rather observe them as thought
they are the clients
my clients my pay check it out
over the shoulder driver rear
view mirror this tip top spasmodic
involuntary victory factory
rings that arm for print-type colour wheels
on the eyes
I'm still not reading
the fetish is write in front of me
but it's so mine I can't ever fix
a strawberry daiquiri without the flashing
lights of public eyes
winding the prickly pear on my own
roll of tape because there's already
other fruit to the jackpot I don't want
know care feel,
the dots behind the word
signify lack
of closure and absolute
desire of affirmation hammer
hitting difference

from my indifference that mulls the combos,
nails the gears
and is so damn dry.

The governed

With the over-bleached smell
of my yellowing panties on burglar bars,
it's such a down-to-earth lease.

My fingers smell anonymous
wiping stripes across your eyes
from just down the road.

Pastoral, with birds blundering into sound.
It could be yourself,
just down the N1 – pop over.

Wander back to where you thought.
Wonder back to wear it.
Either it happens before or after

the sound of the highway –
a whole night on the peninsula
but my driving force doesn't wake me.

The mistress of the mistress

Slave, you say "Mistress"
I cannot command you,
as your finger masters me.

"Your legs" you want to worship
my worthiness to your skin.
I would not know, want to

pleasure
you uselessly.
Neither would you – to me

you confuse with roles
I must manifest in a stereotype.
Slave you, say "Mistress"

you never obey me.
As though you want to be told
to do what you already want.

Slave you say, "Mistress."
I give you permission,
I submit.

Your hand's on my back,
my head's in your leg
and I tell you when I feel it.

Every moment dies

This tirade force
to move me out the reality I asphyxiate
I hyperventilate.
Shallow fast.
In out.
Smear your tongue down
my throat I feel,
little orgasms of life going past.
Not breathing.
Shallowly.
Swallowing.
Don't stop.
I'm coming back
for the eternal return.

Take care of the killer be's

The mood
is one of extrospective heaviness
with a lightness of relevance.

Expect a high pressure of nuance
in the mouth region
with a low pressure moving

across the nether region.
Cool sea breezes will blow offshore
affecting no one.

Maximums are kept in tow
while minimums can drop
below the sheets.

And the bladder
will, as always,
display infrequent showers.

The what of the them and theirs

On these illegal tainted hands
lost now in the smell of rain,
my hair strands dip words.

Switches off the shitness of this train
scrawling illegibly in disgust
long enough to have changed me.

I still get off on being someone else,
I don't change.
I don't know.

I know who I am, I don't know who I be.
Or why.
And how.

Don't know what is.
The hard ass art of belonging
I've lost in this piece of my hiding.

In someone else's world·of work.
There is mine.
But I will drink myself to death distracting myself.

For getting

I

The feathers feel like plastic bubbles.
The humming
murmurs.

My pants.
What an incorrigible waste of time.

I'm not in the lounge anymore, is the problem
when you glare through the sliding doors,
it's not the landlady's peeing
on my cars
that struck me in.

Karma is for if you believe
if you're worthy of such retribution,
and I never was.

A one-book poet
happily going along
to being domestic.

My little blow heater.

I roll my eyeballs.
The back of my head is not ink
filing weighing
dialling
the number
of my fingers,
is more than I can count.

II

Karma is too artificial.
One day everything becomes play.

I did something completely new with my brother.
I took him drinking.
We both wore scared.
I don't know what came over me.

It's quite a nice brink of being. It's performative.

Do we share the space that someone must possess?

You think something else is possible, but it's not
a paper umbrella next to my ashtray.

Sunning desk.
Lamp fixed.
Holiday home.

III

We do this alone together.

It will be just as mundane as it can possibly be.

As soon as you write about it, you play.

It's the lack of heat that is savouring.

At least I know that I'm never going to remember it.

Even if you just imagine what is right there?

Catch the heater with your black and yellow socks.

The contrast is whether it sticks.

IV

I'd like to know that these whims affect me somehow.

It's not any of the expecteds.
What would be the point?
We kissed around the corner.
Foot in your sister's gearbox
moving.

Move the ashtray and the umbrella has more horizon.
Clear, un-shaded.

Work's like going into an incubator –
it's crazy what grows.

Blame it on a playboy bunny

This car rolled back
into the one in front of me.

The front guy got out and demanded
from the white middleclass datsun

his number – no car was damaged
they kept the traffic back

by two lights with their squabble,
the second guy kicked in the door.

I watched with self-society-consciousness
with no licence,

waited patiently
as though life happens to me.

I could be a slut all the time
if things happened to me.

Leaves fall in the water

You notice.
There's no notice on the church door and
fire in my hands.
I raise my body from my morning
to bed I raise myself and leaves are left to stand
in the breath of kisses from my hands.
Handshakes twigging tugs
in the fingerprints of my other tip,
I am still a woman.
I cry.
I am still human.
I cry about everything
and don't feel either.

Where you from?

You can sit alonest in a big city.

In your room you are nowhere.

You are sitting with a glass of wine.
Surrounded by people and populated with longings.

And no one knows.

That you're on big screen at the rugby stadium,
smoking a cigarette.

But you know.

That it was a childish childhood.
Of typical paranoias.

That made you blame your father.

In the dusklands of Plath's mushrooms,
the world subverts you.

Into subversion, you know.

With a hot back and a scratchy bra.

You're just wearing your school uniform, always.

The sun needs attention

Petals falling short of the bin,
she says she likes the leaves changing –
beautiful she says.

Once, her nipple peeped at me from the duvet.
Lying in the sun hungover,
we were giggling in the sublime darkness

of Pollocks her hair mats the carpet
she sweeps
when I'm not looking.

She holds something in her hand –
lined lip purse with zipper smile,
persists with a furrow on her brow,

concentrating her body throws on the carpet
that surprise me
and the poetry she holds to herself,

reading in the garden.
I watch her from my window,
un-tactile,

I watch everything –
unless there's more
to the keys we already share and still manage.

I'm having sex while everyone is dying

The smell of your sweet accidental
sweat my fingers on cold
latex bounded for the top
bus springs my step
bump my head,
I gasp you.
Aren't found on my breast,
riding one stage
to your grin,
lies so close
to everyone laughing.

Dream

Intimate moments are beautiful,
I would like him to lie silently.
and feel my breast.
It would be telepathic,
meeting me out there.
And if I hold him,
will you fly away?

Love poem

Eventually seeking for you was quite hard.
Eventually wanting you was quite dire.
To explain the being of my yearning for.
And to repel the punches of because.
I want a discussion of.
To validate my excuses for my life here.
To feel the excitement of my crisis more.
Of timber-seeking ridicule of the sexes
and fire-starting lividity of waiting.

I don't know
where I am at, why I am doing
this to that,
that to this.
Yesterday and tomorrow,
flowers and whims
and today

take me home and seduce me to being.
Take my heart and feel my clitoris,
because I found it so intriguing the last time.
To secure my lip twitching in my knuckle.
To feel my cold nose for all the time
masked in indulgence but exasperated in release,
I want, rather not anything else.
Except for the humming buzz of lost automobiles,
I breathe infrequently.

I lie myself

I lie sideways in a horizontal patch
below my bookshelf is boxes –
wooden, stacked in formation

around my books forming my idea,
my body of thought
but I lie.

This inverse shadow as though my body is my own,
my clitoris a secret,
the cave wall of Plato,

and think this is mine to foster or grow
in my angular horizontal patch
work path across divans in bedded landscapes,

as though everything is sexual
if my body is my own and
not if it's not.

But it's not like that.

Knowing nothing while doing it

Maybe we are inherently evil,
talking in gruesome hateful subliminal messages
massacring life
with painted-on morals, emotions, feelings, religion:
insincere twits
trying to be what we are not
innately, gaining insecurity
from fear of dying ourselves
we stop others
killing our youth of perception
of existence becoming a hundred metre spring from decay
never being able to do it
in such a small amount of time
as to deny decay
towards ceasing this endless battle
of questions driving us on
wondering if I've said enough,
read enough,
met enough,
cried enough,
expressed enough,
lived enough
not to need to write
like Michelangelo painted the ceiling out
of his commitment to the pope,
demanding social initiative
to keep with the mediocrity
and the altruism of genius
being something we need
to understand
so that you can classify yourself one
in your small slice of the world
weighing on you as Atlas
is the essence of Freud
not being able to figure out
why it bugged us so much,

being annoyed by
complexities, fixating themselves
in eccentricity, driving us on
to find balance in not caring
who you are,
when normal in yourself,
wandering about yourself
with binoculars and pens,
scarring the resonance of the treadmill
of time transporting me away
from these dead legs
I get from reading.

Crazy about the boots, puss

Take a ladle in your pulled mouth,
tongs for rolled eyeballs.
The pot is bigger than a sheep's brain
but who eats grey matter when you can read it.

An Einstein is revived
by fashion I don't wear my pointy boots
in public,
private or in my closet because they're in the shop

I can buy with my eyes
and no pill to cure the therapy,
I put a new tail on my ass with my mind
and the way my shoes make me walk.

Different pairs ask for different days
and different depths of my toes pulling
the leather to stay on I walk
with a sway or sometimes, I hate

to admit always, slippery socks
and a hat that is not cotton
but no one notices.
Except their own bat of an eye swooping

in the dark for your hair.
I buy something I believe
will make me outside
of my cave and gravel

sliding down my pockets
inside my hole,
there echoes wings
pat-patting my femaleness

is only one of them
creatures with horseshoes
pouring the luck under
over, the spikes of decision.

I rub my nose, backhand

I burned incense,
after we smoked the room up.
As though you were a spirit,

that I used to like.
While putting my hairclips in the
mousepad of my laptop.

While you wait

My heart comes slowly unravelled,
tinfoil turns a star.
Light socket needs an electrician
memory told me.
That this will mean nothing.
Who's God – tell me
it's a running joke.
What will move me to write,
to tell?
Not this.